MAKE IT MAKE SENSE™

UNDERSTANDING YOUR INCOME, TAXES, AND EVERYDAY MONEY

Shanae Starnes

Shanae Starnes LLC Publishing

Published by Shanae Starnes LLC Publishing

First Edition 2026

ISBN: 979-8-234-07250-4

Printed in the United States of America

DEDICATION

This book is dedicated to every person who has ever felt confused about money, taxes, and how it all connects.

To those who were never taught but chose to learn anyway.

To those who are building, growing, and becoming more aware of how their decisions shape their future.

And to the next generation, so they can start with understanding instead of confusion.

This is for you.

TABLE OF CONTENTS

ACKNOWLEDGMENTS

This book is a reflection of growth, experience, and the decision to understand what once felt confusing.

First, I give thanks to God for guidance, clarity, and the ability to continue learning and teaching. Every step of this journey has required faith, patience, and the willingness to move forward even when I did not have all the answers.

To my family, thank you for your support, your patience, and your presence. Your encouragement has allowed me to continue building, growing, and stepping into new levels of purpose.

To my children, you are a constant reminder of why understanding matters. Everything I learn, build, and teach is rooted in creating better opportunities, clearer paths, and stronger foundations for the next generation.

To the individuals I have worked with over the years—clients, students, and professionals—thank you. Your questions, your experiences, and your desire to understand more have helped shape the way I teach and communicate. You are the reason this book exists.

To the mentors, educators, and programs that have contributed to my journey, I appreciate the knowledge that has been shared. Each lesson added a layer of understanding that I now pass on to others.

This book was created for anyone who has ever felt confused about money, taxes, and how it all connects. It is for those who are ready to move from guessing to understanding.

Thank you for being here, for choosing to learn, and for allowing me to be a part of your journey.

Let's continue to grow, learn, and make it make sense.

INTRODUCTION

At some point, most people realize that something about money and taxes just does not feel clear. You earn, you spend, you file, and somehow the outcome still feels confusing.

You may have asked yourself questions like:

Why do I owe?

Why didn't I get back what I expected?

How does this even work?

And the truth is, those questions are valid.

Because most people were never taught how to connect what they do every day with how taxes actually work.

They were taught how to earn money.

They were taught how to pay bills.

But they were not taught how income is viewed, how decisions impact outcomes, or how to move with intention throughout the year.

That gap is what creates confusion.

This book was created to close that gap.

My journey into understanding taxes did not come from knowing everything at the beginning. It came from stepping into spaces where I had to learn, ask questions, and apply what I was being taught in real time.

Over the years, I have worked with individuals from different backgrounds—employees, entrepreneurs, beauty professionals, and independent contractors—many of whom shared the same experience. They were doing the work, earning income, and showing up in their lives, but they did not fully understand how everything connected.

What I realized is this.

It is not that people are incapable of understanding taxes. It is that the information has not been presented in a way that connects to their everyday life.

This book is not about memorizing rules or overwhelming you with information.

It is about helping you see clearly.

It is about helping you understand how your income works, how your decisions impact your results, and how to move from confusion to awareness.

You will not find complicated language here. You will not find information that assumes you already know everything.

What you will find is a way to break things down, step by step, in a way that allows you to think differently about money and taxes.

This is not about being perfect.

It is about becoming aware.

Because once you understand what is happening, you stop guessing.

And once you stop guessing, you start making decisions with intention.

That is where the shift happens.

This book is your starting point.

And from here, everything begins to make more sense.

ABOUT THE AUTHOR

Shanae Starnes is an educator, entrepreneur, and financial literacy advocate with a passion for helping individuals understand how money, taxes, and everyday decisions are connected.

With over a decade of experience in tax preparation, education, and client consulting, she has worked with individuals from all walks of life, including employees, entrepreneurs, independent contractors, and beauty professionals who are navigating income, business, and financial growth.

Known for her ability to break down complex topics into clear, relatable, and practical conversations, Shanae has built her approach around one core principle: understanding creates confidence.

Her work extends beyond taxes. As a Licensed Career and Technical Education instructor, she has dedicated her career to teaching real-world skills that empower individuals to think critically, make informed decisions, and build sustainable paths for themselves and their families.

Through her training programs, workshops, and educational platforms, she continues to bridge the gap between knowledge and application, helping people move from confusion to clarity in their financial lives.

She is also the founder of Shanae Starnes LLC Publishing, a platform created to provide accessible, practical education that connects everyday life to real financial understanding.

This book represents her commitment to helping others see clearly, think differently, and take ownership of their financial journey.

Because once you understand how it works, you can move with intention.

Chapter 1

WHY TAXES MATTER MORE THAN YOU THINK

Most people don't think about taxes until it's time to file. They gather their documents, sit down, and hope for the best. Some are hoping for a refund. Some are hoping they don't owe. And almost everyone is asking the same question: why does this feel so confusing?

Here's what people don't realize.

Taxes are not something that just shows up once a year. Taxes are happening every time you earn money. Every paycheck. Every client. Every transaction. If you don't understand what's happening in those moments, then tax season will always feel like a surprise.

The real issue is not that taxes are too complicated. The issue is that most people were never taught how to connect their everyday life to their taxes. You were taught how to go to work, earn money, and pay bills. But you were not taught how your income is categorized, how taxes are calculated, or why you owe or receive money back.

So what happens is simple. You participate in a system without understanding how the system works. And that's where frustration begins.

Let's break this down using something familiar. The word is MONEY.

M stands for manage. Money is not just something you receive. It is something you manage. If you are not managing your money throughout the year, then you are leaving your outcome up to chance. Think about it. You receive income regularly, but you are not tracking it, not thinking about taxes, and simply spending what comes in. Then tax time comes and you are trying to figure everything out all at once. That is not management. That is reaction.

O stands for options. Not all money is treated the same. You have options in how you earn, structure, and report your income. Some people earn W-2 income as employees. Others earn 1099 income as independent contractors. Some operate businesses. Some have multiple streams. Each of these options comes with different rules and different tax treatment. Two people can make the same amount of money and have completely different tax outcomes simply because of how their income is structured.

N stands for navigate. Once you understand how money and taxes work, you begin to move differently. You stop asking why something happened and start asking how to prepare for it. You begin to think ahead, set money aside, track income intentionally, and make better decisions during the year instead of reacting at the end of it.

E stands for educate. Knowledge changes everything, but only when you truly understand it. You may have heard phrases like "write it off" or "you'll get a refund," but without understanding what those statements actually mean, you are just repeating information without clarity. Real education is understanding why something works, not just hearing that it does.

Y stands for you. At the end of the day, this is about you. Your income, your choices, your habits, and your awareness. No one cares more about your financial life than you do. And once you take ownership of that, everything begins to shift.

Take a moment and think about your own experience. Have you ever been surprised at tax time? Expected a refund and didn't get one? Owed and didn't understand why? That doesn't mean you did something wrong. It means something wasn't explained.

The truth most people miss is that taxes are not just about filing a return. They are about understanding how your money moves. When you don't understand that, you stay in a cycle of confusion, guessing, and reacting.

So here is your starting point. You don't have to know everything today, but you do need to start paying attention. Pay attention to how you earn. Notice what is being taken out or not taken out. Ask questions when something doesn't make sense. Stop waiting until tax time to think about taxes.

This book is not here to overwhelm you. It is here to help you see things differently. Because once you understand how your money works, you stop being surprised and you start being intentional.

Chapter 2

Understanding Where Your Money Comes From

Most people think money is simple. You get paid, you deposit it, and you spend it. That feels straightforward. But when it comes to taxes, that is only the beginning.

Here's what people don't realize.

Not all money is treated the same. Where your money comes from determines how it is taxed. If you don't understand that, you will always feel confused when it is time to file your taxes. You are not just dealing with money. You are dealing with different types of income.

There are different ways money shows up in your life. You may have a job. You may do work on the side. You may sell products or services. You may have multiple streams of income coming in. On the surface, it all feels the same because it is all money. But behind the scenes, it is being treated very differently.

That difference affects what is taken out, what you are responsible for, and what you may owe later. If you don't understand this early, you will feel like your numbers don't make sense later.

Let's break this down using the word INCOME.

I stands for identify your sources. Before anything else, you need to know where your money is coming from. You cannot understand your taxes if you do not understand your income. Ask yourself if you have a job, if you earn money outside of your job, or if you have multiple ways that you get paid.

For example, you may work a full-time job, but you also do hair, drive for a service, sell products, or offer services. That means you have more than one source of income. Each one matters, even the ones that feel small. When you begin to identify your income sources, you start to see the full picture of your financial life.

N stands for note how it is taxed. Once you identify your income sources, the next step is understanding how each one is taxed. Some income has taxes taken out before you receive it. Other income does not have anything taken out at all.

For example, at a job, taxes are automatically taken out of your paycheck. You receive what is left. But with side income or independent work, you often receive the full amount. That may feel good in the moment, but it creates responsibility later.

Think about this. You earn eight hundred dollars from your job and eight hundred dollars from a side hustle. Those are not the same eight hundred dollars. One has already had taxes taken out. The other has not. If you treat them the same, you will feel confused later.

C stands for categorize it properly. Income is not just about receiving money. It is about how that money is classified. Some income is employee income. Some is independent contractor income. Some is business income. The classification determines how it is treated for tax purposes.

Here's what people don't realize. If income is categorized incorrectly or misunderstood, everything after that becomes confusing. Taxes follow classification. So if you are working independently but thinking like an employee, you may not prepare properly for what comes next.

O stands for organize your records. Most people do not track their income consistently. They rely on memory, bank statements, or last-minute organizing. That creates stress and confusion.

If you are not organizing your income as it comes in, you are setting yourself up to guess later. Imagine earning money throughout the year but not tracking it weekly or monthly. When it is time to file your taxes, you are trying to piece everything together at once. That is overwhelming, but it is also avoidable.

M stands for manage your responsibility. The more control you have over your income, the more responsibility you take on. When you work for someone else, much of the process is handled for you. But when you earn money on your own, you are responsible for tracking it, understanding it, and preparing for it.

Freedom and responsibility go together. If you have the freedom to earn in different ways, you also have the responsibility to manage what comes with it.

E stands for evaluate the impact. Now you bring everything together. Ask yourself how your income is affecting your taxes. Not just how much you made, but how it is being treated and what it means for your future.

Think about your own experience. Have you ever earned extra money, felt good about it, and then felt confused at tax time? That is not random. That is a result of not understanding how your income was being handled.

So here is your new approach. Identify all your income sources. Understand how each one is taxed. Track your income consistently. Think ahead instead of waiting until tax time.

Money is not just about what you receive. It is about what you understand. And once you understand your income, everything else begins to make more sense.

Chapter 3

Understanding How Much You Really Earn

Most people can tell you how much they make. They'll say things like "I make fifty thousand a year" or "I brought in sixty thousand." On the surface, that sounds clear and straightforward.

Here's what people don't realize.

What you make is not always what you are taxed on. There is a difference between what you earn and what actually counts when your taxes are calculated. If you do not understand that difference, your results will always feel confusing.

Between the moment you earn money and the moment taxes are calculated, there are layers. These layers determine what is included, what is reduced, and what is ultimately taxed. So when you say you made a certain amount of money, that is only the starting point, not the final number.

Let's break this down using the word EARN.

E stands for evaluate your gross income. Your gross income is everything you earned before anything is taken out. This includes your paycheck before taxes, your side income, your business income, and any other money that came in.

For example, you may earn forty-five thousand dollars from your job and an additional ten thousand dollars from side work. That means your total gross income is fifty-five thousand dollars. This is your starting number. It gives you a full picture of what came in during the year, but it is not what you will necessarily be taxed on.

A stands for adjust what counts.

Here's what people don't realize. Not all of your income stays the same when it comes time to calculate taxes. There are things that can reduce your income before it is taxed. These are called adjustments.

Adjustments can come from certain types of expenses, contributions, or other qualifying factors. The key point is that these adjustments lower the amount of income that is considered when your taxes are calculated.

For example, if your total income is fifty-five thousand dollars, adjustments may reduce that number. You might not be taxed on the full fifty-five thousand. Instead, your taxable amount could be lower depending on what applies to your situation.

This is where many people begin to feel confused because they are still thinking in terms of what they earned instead of what is being counted.

R stands for recognize taxable versus non-taxable income.

Not all money is treated the same way. Some income is fully taxable. Some income is partially taxable. Some income may not be taxable at all depending on the situation.

If you do not recognize the difference, you may assume that everything is treated the same. That can lead to overestimating what you owe or misunderstanding your financial situation.

Understanding how your income behaves helps you interpret your results more clearly.

For example, if you receive different types of income throughout the year but treat them all the same, you may not understand why your final numbers look the way they do. Once you begin to recognize the differences, things start to make more sense.

N stands for notice the difference.

This is where everything starts to connect. There is a difference between your gross income, your adjusted income, and your taxable income.

Gross income is what you earned. Adjusted income reflects reductions that apply before taxes are calculated. Taxable income is the amount that is actually used to determine what you owe.

For example, you may earn fifty thousand dollars, but after adjustments and reductions, you may only be taxed on forty-two thousand dollars. That difference is the reason outcomes vary. It is the reason some people owe less, some receive refunds, and some are surprised by the results.

Think about your own experience.

Have you ever looked at your income and felt confident, only to feel confused when your taxes were calculated?

That is not random. It is the result of not understanding the layers between earning and taxation.

Common mistakes happen in this area.

One mistake is thinking all income is taxed the same way. Another is focusing only on what you made instead of what is taxable. Another is ignoring adjustments because you did not know they existed. And one of the biggest mistakes is waiting until tax time to try to understand everything at once.

So here is your new approach.

Instead of saying “I made this much,” start asking “What is my taxable income?” Ask what adjustments apply to you. Ask what is actually being counted.

Understanding your income is not just about numbers. It is about awareness.

Once you understand how your income is viewed, you stop being confused by the outcome and you start seeing the process clearly.

Chapter 4

WHAT REDUCES YOUR TAXES

At some point, almost everyone asks the same question: how do I pay less in taxes?

Once that question comes up, you start hearing things like "write it off," "track your expenses," or "you can claim that." It starts to sound like there are easy ways to lower what you owe.

Here's what people don't realize.

Not everything reduces your taxes the way you think it does. And if you do not understand how it actually works, you may believe you are saving money when you are not.

There are things that reduce the amount of income that gets taxed, and there are things that reduce what you actually owe. This chapter focuses on the first part, which is what reduces your taxable income.

Before you can understand your final number, you need to understand what happens in the middle.

Let's break this down using the word SAVE.

S stands for see your deductions.

Deductions reduce your taxable income. That means they lower the amount of money the IRS looks at when calculating your taxes.

For example, if you earn fifty thousand dollars and have five thousand dollars in deductions, you are now taxed on forty-five thousand dollars instead of the full amount. That helps, but it does not reduce your tax bill dollar for dollar.

This is where people get confused. They think a deduction works like a direct payment toward what they owe, but it does not. It simply lowers the amount of income being taxed.

A stands for apply them correctly.

Not everything you spend money on is deductible. Just because you spent money does not mean it qualifies.

There has to be a clear connection between the expense and how you earn your income. If that connection is not there, the expense may not apply.

For example, someone may buy something and assume they can write it off without understanding whether it is necessary or related to their income. That assumption can create problems later.

Applying deductions correctly means understanding why something qualifies, not just assuming that it does.

V stands for verify eligibility.

What works for someone else may not work for you. You may hear advice from others about what they claim or what they can write off, but their situation may be different.

Their income structure, their business setup, and their financial situation all play a role in what applies to them. That means you cannot simply copy what someone else is doing and expect the same result.

You have to verify what applies to your situation.

E stands for evaluate the impact.

Not all deductions have the same effect. Some reduce your taxable income slightly, while others may have a larger impact.

Here's what people don't realize. Spending money does not automatically mean you are saving money on your taxes.

For example, if you spend one thousand dollars and that amount qualifies as a deduction, it reduces your taxable income. It does not mean you receive one thousand dollars back.

The actual impact depends on how that deduction affects your taxable income, not just the amount you spent.

This is why it is important to understand what a deduction is actually doing instead of assuming the outcome.

Think about your own experience.

Have you ever spent money thinking it would help you at tax time, only to feel like the result did not match your expectation?

That is usually not because something went wrong. It is because something was misunderstood.

There are common mistakes in this area.

One mistake is thinking every expense is deductible. Another is spending money just to try to reduce taxes. Another is not tracking expenses consistently throughout the year. And another is confusing deductions with credits, which work differently.

When you do not track your expenses as they happen, you end up trying to remember everything at once later. That creates stress and increases the chance of mistakes.

So here is your new approach.

Track your expenses as they happen. Keep your system simple and consistent. Understand what qualifies and why it qualifies. Ask questions instead of assuming. And always evaluate the actual impact instead of focusing only on the activity.

You do not need to spend more or do more. You need to understand more.

Because once you understand how deductions work, you stop trying to guess your way through it and start making decisions that actually make sense.

Chapter 5

CREDITS VS. DEDUCTIONS — WHAT REALLY LOWERS YOUR TAXES

At some point, almost everyone asks the same question: how do I lower what I owe?

Once that question comes up, you start hearing things like "write it off," "claim this," or "you'll get more back." It can sound like there are simple ways to reduce your taxes.

Here's what people don't realize.

Not everything that sounds helpful works the same way. There are two different things happening when it comes to lowering your taxes. One reduces your income. The other reduces what you actually owe.

If you do not understand the difference, you may expect one result and get another.

Let's slow this down.

Deductions reduce your taxable income. Credits reduce your actual tax bill. That difference may sound small, but the impact is very different.

Let's break this down using the word LESS.

L stands for lower your income.

Deductions lower the amount of income that is taxed. For example, if you earn fifty thousand dollars and have five thousand dollars in deductions, you are now taxed on forty-five thousand dollars instead of the full amount.

That helps, but it does not directly reduce your tax bill dollar for dollar. It only reduces the amount of income being used to calculate your taxes.

This is where many people misunderstand how deductions work. They hear that something can be written off and assume it means they will not have to pay as much, without understanding how the reduction actually happens.

E stands for eliminate what you owe.

Credits work differently. Credits reduce your actual tax bill. For example, if you owe two thousand dollars in taxes and qualify for a one thousand dollar credit, your new balance is one thousand dollars.

That is a direct reduction. This is why credits often feel more impactful. They affect what you owe after your taxes have been calculated.

S stands for see the difference.

This is where clarity begins. When people hear "you can write that off," they often assume that it will significantly reduce what they owe. But without understanding whether something is a deduction or a credit, it is easy to misunderstand the outcome.

Seeing the difference between the two allows you to understand what is actually happening instead of relying on assumptions.

S stands for strategize your outcome.

Once you understand how deductions and credits work, you begin to think differently. Instead of asking what you can write off, you begin asking better questions.

You start asking what reduces your income, what reduces what you owe, and what actually applies to your situation. That shift in thinking leads to better decisions.

Think about a real-life situation.

Two people earn the same amount of money. One has deductions that lower their taxable income. The other qualifies for credits that reduce what they owe. Even though they started at the same place, their outcomes may feel very different.

Another example is when someone spends money thinking it will help them on their taxes. They may believe that spending one thousand dollars means they will get one thousand dollars back. In reality, that amount only reduces their taxable income, not their tax bill directly.

This is why it is important to understand what each action is actually doing.

There are common mistakes in this area.

One mistake is spending money just to try to create deductions. Another is thinking deductions and credits are the same. Another is not knowing what you actually qualify for. And another is expecting a certain outcome without understanding the numbers behind it.

When these misunderstandings happen, people feel like their taxes do not make sense. But the issue is not the outcome. The issue is the lack of clarity around how the system works.

So here is your new approach.

Instead of asking what you can write off, ask what reduces your income and what reduces what you owe. Ask how each one impacts your situation. Focus on understanding, not just the result.

Lowering your taxes is not about doing more. It is about understanding better.

Once you understand the difference between deductions and credits, you stop guessing and start making decisions that actually make sense.

Chapter 6

SELF-EMPLOYMENT & RESPONSIBILITY — WHEN YOU BECOME THE SYSTEM

There is a moment that feels really good. It is the moment when you start making your own money.

Maybe you pick up a side hustle. Maybe you start doing hair, nails, or services. Maybe you begin selling, consulting, or creating. And the first thought is simple. You made this on your own.

That feels empowering.

Here's what people don't realize.

When you make your own money, you also take on your own responsibility.

When you work a job, taxes are taken out for you. Your income is tracked. The system is already in place. You are operating within a structure that handles most of the process behind the scenes.

But when you step into self-employment, you become the system.

If you do not understand that shift, that is where confusion begins.

Let's look at the difference more clearly.

As an employee, you receive income after taxes have already been taken out. Your employer handles most of the reporting and tracking. You are part of an established process.

As a self-employed individual, you receive income before taxes. You are responsible for tracking it. You are responsible for reporting it. You are responsible for understanding how it all works.

That is a completely different experience.

Let's break this down using the word BIZ.

B stands for build your income.

Self-employment gives you the ability to earn more and create opportunities. You are not limited to one stream. You can expand your income based on your effort, your skills, and your strategy.

But here is what people don't realize. More income does not automatically mean more understanding.

You can be making more money and still feel confused at tax time if you are not paying attention to what is happening behind the scenes.

For example, you may start earning money on the side. Clients are paying you, money is coming in, and you feel like you are growing. But you are not tracking consistently. You are not thinking about taxes. You are not preparing ahead.

That creates a gap between what you are earning and what you understand.

I stands for identify your expenses.

This is one of the advantages of self-employment. You can track expenses that are connected to how you earn your income.

These may include supplies, equipment, tools, or other necessary purchases related to your work.

Here's what people don't realize. Expenses only help you if they are tracked properly.

They must be necessary, connected to your income, and documented. If they are not tracked, they cannot be used effectively.

For example, you may spend money on products, tools, or services related to your work. If you do not track those expenses, you may end up being taxed on the full amount you earned instead of what you actually kept.

That leads to confusion and frustration, but it is preventable with consistency.

Z stands for zero in on your profit.

This is one of the most important concepts to understand.

Profit is the difference between what you earn and what you spend.

If you earn fifty thousand dollars and have fifteen thousand dollars in expenses, your profit is closer to thirty-five thousand dollars.

Here's what people don't realize. You are not taxed on everything you make. You are taxed on what remains after your expenses.

That difference matters. It changes how you think about your income and how you prepare for taxes.

If you only focus on what you earned and ignore your expenses, you may misunderstand your situation.

There are common mistakes in this area.

One mistake is not tracking income consistently. Another is mixing personal and business money, which creates confusion. Another is waiting until tax time to organize everything. And another is assuming someone else will handle it.

When you are self-employed, you are responsible. That is not something to be afraid of, but it is something to understand.

Think about your own experience.

Have you ever made money on the side and not tracked it fully? Have you felt unsure about what to report? Have you waited until the last minute to organize everything?

That is common, but now you understand why it matters.

So here is your new approach.

Track your income weekly. Record your expenses consistently. Separate your business and personal money. Think ahead instead of reacting at tax time.

Self-employment is not just about making money. It is about managing money.

Once you understand that, you stop feeling overwhelmed and start feeling in control.

You do not have to know everything right now, but you do need to take ownership.

Because when you understand your role, you stop guessing and start operating with intention.

Chapter 7

COMMON MISTAKES — WHAT COSTS YOU WITHOUT YOU REALIZING IT

Most people do not set out to make mistakes on their taxes. They are not trying to do anything wrong. They are simply trying to get through the process and move on.

But mistakes still happen.

Here's what people don't realize.

Most tax mistakes do not come from carelessness. They come from not understanding, not tracking, or making assumptions.

And the cost of those mistakes is not always immediate.

Sometimes it shows up as owing unexpectedly. Sometimes it shows up as getting less than expected. And sometimes it shows up as feeling confused year after year.

The real issue is not just the mistake itself. The issue is not knowing why it happened.

Because when you do not understand the cause, you repeat the cycle.

Let's break this down using the word ERROR.

E stands for excluding income.

This happens more often than people think.

If you earn money, it needs to be accounted for. Even if it was a small amount. Even if it was not consistent. Even if you did not receive a form.

For example, you may do a few side jobs, receive cash payments, or earn money through apps. It may not feel like a lot in the moment, but over time it adds up.

If that income is not tracked, it creates gaps in your reporting and confusion in your results.

R stands for reporting incorrectly.

Even when people try to do things the right way, mistakes can happen.

This may include entering numbers incorrectly, mislabeling income, or missing important details. Small errors can lead to delays, notices, or confusion later.

Accuracy matters. Taking your time and checking your work can prevent many of these issues.

R stands for rushing the process.

This is one of the most common problems.

When people sit down to do their taxes, they often just want to get it done. They rush through the process without fully understanding what they are doing.

When you rush, you miss details. You overlook opportunities. You skip understanding.

Later, when something feels off, it is harder to go back and figure out what happened.

O stands for overclaiming.

This happens when people try to claim things that do not qualify or do not apply to their situation.

Sometimes it comes from hearing advice from others. Someone may say you can write something off, and you assume it applies to you without fully understanding the rules.

But not everything qualifies, and not everything applies to every situation.

Claiming something without understanding it can create problems later.

R stands for repeating patterns.

This is what keeps people stuck.

The same mistakes happen year after year, not because people cannot learn, but because they do not take the time to understand what went wrong.

Think about your own experience.

Have you ever said that the same thing happened last year? Have you ever felt like you were going through the same confusion again?

That is a pattern.

Breaking that pattern starts with awareness.

Mistakes are not the real problem. Unawareness is.

Once you understand what went wrong, why it happened, and what to do differently, you break the cycle.

So here is your new approach.

Instead of focusing on the mistake, focus on the lesson. Ask yourself what you learned, what you can do differently next time, and what you understand now that you did not before.

You do not have to be perfect. You just have to be aware.

Because awareness leads to better decisions, more confidence, and less confusion.

And over time, it leads to consistency.

Mistakes do not define you. They guide you, if you are willing to pay attention.

Once you understand that, you stop repeating the same story and start writing a new one.

Chapter 8

FROM KNOWLEDGE TO ACTION – MAKING IT MAKE SENSE IN YOUR LIFE

You have made it this far. You have learned about income, how it is taxed, what reduces it, what impacts what you owe, and the mistakes to avoid.

At this point, you might be thinking that you understand more than you did before.

That is a good place to be.

Here's what people don't realize.

Understanding something once does not change your life. What changes your life is what you do with what you understand.

Knowledge without action becomes information that is forgotten. That is not what this book is for.

This is where the shift happens.

Up until now, you have been learning. Now it is time to start applying what you have learned.

Taxes are not something that only show up once a year. They are something you interact with all year long.

Every time you earn, spend, decide, or plan, you are influencing your outcome.

Let's bring everything together using the word GROW.

G stands for gain awareness.

You are now more aware than you were before. You understand that income is not all the same. You understand that what you earn is not always what you are taxed on. You understand that deductions and credits work differently. You understand that responsibility increases as your control increases.

Most people never reach this level of awareness. They stay in a cycle of confusion, guessing, and reacting.

But now you see things differently.

R stands for review your habits.

This is the moment where you look at your own behavior honestly.

Ask yourself how you have been managing your money. Ask yourself if you have been tracking consistently. Ask yourself if you truly understand your income sources.

You may realize that you have been guessing, waiting until tax time, or hoping everything works out. That is not judgment. That is awareness.

O stands for organize your finances.

Understanding is powerful, but organization is what makes it real.

You do not need a complicated system. You need a consistent one.

This can look like tracking your income weekly, keeping your expenses recorded, separating your business and personal money, and staying organized throughout the year.

Two people can earn the same amount of money, but the one who is organized will have a completely different experience than the one who waits until the last minute.

W stands for work with intention.

This is where everything shifts.

Instead of reacting to what happens, you begin to move with purpose.

You start asking how your decisions today will affect you later. You start thinking ahead instead of just responding in the moment. You begin making choices based on understanding instead of assumption.

Intentional decisions create different outcomes.

Think about your journey.

Before this, you may have felt unsure. You may have guessed. You may have relied on others to explain things to you.

Now you understand more, and that matters.

Taxes are not just about filing a return, getting a refund, or paying what you owe. They are connected to your entire financial life.

Your income, your choices, your habits, and your growth all play a role.

Once you understand that, you stop seeing taxes as a burden and start seeing them as a system you can learn and manage.

From here, you have options.

You can continue learning. You can apply what you understand. You can improve your habits over time. You can seek guidance when you need it.

Or you can take it a step further.

Understanding your taxes is one level. Learning how to prepare taxes is another.

For some, that becomes a skill that creates income and opportunity.

If you are interested in learning how to prepare tax returns, understand real scenarios, build a skill you can use, and create income from what you know, that opportunity is available to you.

This book was not created to make you an expert overnight.

It was created to help you see clearly, think differently, and move with intention.

Now when you hear someone say that taxes do not make sense, you will be able to say something different.

You will be able to say, let's make it make sense.

www.ingramcontent.com/pod-product-compliance
Lightning Source LLC
LaVergne TN
LVHW020312110826
845148LV00017BA/2641
979823407250 4